Coronavirus Haiku

Coronavirus Haiku

Poetry to Help Lighten your Pandemic Days

James Weir

Reg'n No 1169543
ISBN 978-1-7772280-1-9

Dedicated to
Leslie, Annie and Sultan
Locked up together

Sickly coughing bat
Gets revenge at the market
Pandemic panic

Coronavirus
Five syllables to rhyme with
Bad haiku follows

Isolation time
Time to reflect and to grow….
Or spy on neighbors

Streets are all empty
Pandemic Apocalypse
Actually, it's nice!

Social distancing
I have experience of that
At the high school dance

My peace is shattered
Neighbors' kids are screaming loud
Fucking rats from hell

Pandemic Task Force
Trump not a stable genius
Why can't HE drink bleach?

I can’t buy a mask
I don’t know what I will use
Strap on maxi-pad?

It's COVID-19
Sounds like a bad rapper's name
Won't download those songs

Nothing left to eat
Peanut butter on a spoon
Quarantine fifteen

God I am so bored
Alphabetized the spice rack
When will this all end?

Netflix keeps me sane
Binging helps me to escape
Tiger King is weird

Work meeting on Zoom
Bob has got no boxers on
Cannot unsee this

Neighbors' kids are loose
Mixing together outside
Bioreactors

Locked in with hubby
Scraping fork drives me insane
Breathing much too loud

The rich are locked up
Posting pics of their huge yacht
Tone deaf very much?

Government sets rules
"Stay at home and don't go out"
Jared? Ivanka?

Home schooling for now
I don't remember this math
My kid will be doomed

Amazon driver
Bringing all the essentials
Like the new dildo

Neighbor's smoking weed
It's stinking up my whole house
Indoor hot-box high

Orange Dumbass shouts
"Fake News. Fake News. I'm the best"
Again, please drink bleach

Virus on groceries
Sanitize and sanitize
My chips taste like soap

Always washing hands
Scrubbing them until they're raw
Knuckles bleeding now

Zig-zag on a walk
Avoiding viral muggers
The new self-defense

Cough into your sleeve
Thanks god virus not G.I.
Can’t shit in elbow

Talk show host hates Zoom
At least she has an income
What a whining jerk

Watching old movies
The movies that shaped my life
Those movies were crap

Around the clock news
Pandemic goes on and on
Bad news on repeat

Internet is down
Guess I'll go and read a book
Can't – forgot how to

Toilet paper gone
How to wipe my dirty ass?
Cat smells funny now

Orange Dumbass exalts
"Hydroxychloroquine saves"
Snake oil in a pill

Small treats make one's day
"Did you eat the last donut?"
Sleeping on the couch

Protestors want out
Open the economy
Bye Bye to Granny…

I miss petting dogs
Biohazards with soft fur
Harshes my mellow

Can't go to the spa
Lady scaping suffering
Not pretty down there

It was in the news
Cats get coronavirus
Good. The cat hates me

Couples fighting more
Isolation makes them crack
Six feet not enough

No sports on TV
People need entertainment
Athletes get tests first

Wartime President
You are not a Roosevelt
I miss Obama

The Covidiots
Jammed together at the beach
Set phasers on “stunned”

Religious freedom
Go ahead and go to church
Meet Jesus sooner

Seven syllables
Epidemiologist
Couldn't be more cool

“Stop touching your face
Do it again and you’re out”
Sleeping in my car

Watching my neighbors
Never noticed that lady
Ugly femullet

Snuggled on the couch
Keeping warm under blankets
Dutch oven NOT cool

Long-haul truckers rock
But nowhere for them to poop
Use my neighbor’s lawn

A cough at the store
Heads all turn at once and look
And scatter away

I can't find this stuff
Clorox. Lysol. Sanitizer.
The new black market

All this home schooling
Kids constantly online now
Pedophiles in bliss

Old man at the store
Stopped in doorway checking list
Step aside fuckwad

Taking precautions
Tried microwaving the mail
Fire is out now

Neighbors gather close
Social distancing my ass
Gonna rat them out

House has a real stink
It smells like a skunk's asshole
Oh, it's me. My bad

Wearing the same clothes
Laundry doesn't seem worthwhile
Dog won't sit with me

Differing opinions
From too much togetherness
Farts no longer fun

People are horny
Skyping ‘friends with benefits’
Doesn’t seem the same

COVID kills more men
A cosmic “bros before hos”
Women win this one

Poor Doctor Fauci
Stressed out by Orange Dumbass
Brad Pitt thinks you’re cool

My hair keeps growing
Looking like a rock star now
Solely in my mind

Getting outside now
Cyclists breeze through the stop signs
They're all still assholes

Keeping my distance
She cuts in front to get milk
I hope you die soon

Getting my takeout
Guy at counter looks like shit
This food will kill me

Social media
Touting bad advice to all
Go back in your hole

Haircut needed now
Cut my own in the mirror
It will grow back soon….

House cleaning has stopped
Things are getting out of hand
Whose skid mark is that?

Long-term care virus
Creating new vacancies
Can't make this funny

Economy downturns
No industry growth in site
Except funerals

UK slow response
Boris Johnson gets COVID
Karma IS a bitch

Telecommuting now
Staying home and keeping safe
Boss is still a jerk

Slaughterhouse virus
"Keep them open at all costs!"
The pigs disagree

Quarantine fifteen
"Did you put on some weight honey?"
Sleeping in my car

"LIBERATE the States
Open the economy!"
Dumbass kills his base

Trying to stay sane
Jigsaw puzzles pass the time
Dog ate the last piece

Not wearing clothes now
Squirrel-out but I don't care
Neighbors called the cops

Chip bags on the floor
Dishes piled up in the sink
Depression ensues

Celebs are streaming
Advice that no one asked for
They're attention whores

Cabin fever soars
Emotions raw and ragged
Hangry gets intense

Toilet paper in stock
A riot in the aisles
They died for two-ply

They shout "Let us Out"
"It's our American right!"
Gene pool needs chlorine

Lost in thoughts again
Write book of virus haiku?
Nah, that's for losers

Coughing in the house
Find a hairball on my bed
The cat still hates me

Watching for fever
The thermometer tastes weird
Where's the oral one?

Having vivid dreams
Therapists say its normal
Scary none-the-less

A branding failure
Corona beer as a name
Sorry for your luck

PPE is rare
Shortages abound for all
Outsourcing was bad

Bills are piling up
Don’t know how I will manage
Time to sell the cat

Coronavirus
Picture looks like ball with spikes
Microscopic flail

Everything online
Deliveries are lifeline
Driver rings then runs

Confinement must end
Even the dogs want their space
Cat seems more pissed-off

Flattening the curve
We need to cooperate
Sadly, I have doubts

Veterinary
Epidemiologist
Haiku writes itself

Vaccine needed now
Immunity means freedom
Anti-vaxers heed

Why should I worry?
A ventilator shortage?
Use my leaf blower

Silent spreaders roam
Like zombies, sowing virus
Wear your fucking mask

Dearest Porch Pirates:
Special place in hell for you
Hope you too die soon

"God will protect me"
Will you socially distance
At the Pearly Gates?

"I never get sick
I don't need to stay away"
Go lick the doorknob

Tension is rising
Everything is grating now
No "pull my finger"

Mortgage deferment
Payments will be extended
Done next century

Sourdough baking
Flour and make-your-own yeast
Tastes like hockey puck

Use ventilation?
Or not use ventilation?
That is the question

Take-out food again
Dog licks gravy from my shirt
Self-esteem lowers

Zoom lets us observe
Into others' homes and lives
Note – better hide porn

COVID cases mount
US first but Russia gains
The new cold war

Trying to fill time
Belching contest escalates
“Get any on ya?”

Drive-in theaters
The new normal to gather
Now make-out at church

Nasal swabs from hell
Probing the back of my brain
Bad things grow from there

Frontline workers rock!
Working to keep us all safe
Stay home for them please

My job has vanished
Maybe I'll write some haiku
Thanks for buying this

GLOSSARY OF TERMS

Dumbass	**= President Donald J Trump**
Ivanka	**= Dumbass' daughter**
Jared	**= Dumbass' Son-in-Law**
Orange Dumbass	**= see Dumbass**

Other Titles by James Weir:

Asshole Haiku
'Celebrating' The Assholes in Our Everyday Lives

Cat Haiku
Funny Poems About The Lion in the House

Dog Haiku
Funny Poems About Man's Best Friend

ABOUT THE AUTHOR

When he's not busy being a poet (and we use the term poet very loosely here), James Weir is a small animal veterinarian. In addition to clinical practice, he holds graduate degrees in pathology and in public health. He has also worked as a stand-up comedian. He has been published before, but mostly boring science crap. This is his first book of poetry (again, we use this term very loosely).

www.ingramcontent.com/pod-product-compliance
Lightning Source LLC
Chambersburg PA
CBHW031348060726
47590CB00007B/2675

* 9 7 8 1 7 7 7 2 2 8 0 1 9 *